PRAYERS
OF INTERCESSION

SUSAN SAYERS

Kevin
Mayhew

First published in 1997
This revised edition published in 2000 by
KEVIN MAYHEW LTD
Buxhall
Stowmarket
Suffolk IP14 3BW

Prayers of Intercession is extracted from
Living Stones – Complete Resource Book

ISBN 1 84003 013 5
Catalogue No 1500117

Cover photograph courtesy of
Images Colour Library, London
Cover design by Jaquetta Sergeant
Edited by Katherine Laidler
Typesetting by Louise Selfe
Printed and bound in Great Britain

FOREWORD

A praying church is a living organism, powered by the love of God, and directed by his will. The aim of those leading intercessions in public worship is to provide a suitable climate for prayer, both for the faithful core of praying members, and also for those who drift in as visitors, sometimes willingly and sometimes rather grudgingly.

Since our God is in a far better position to know the needs of each muddle of people who arrive on any particular Sunday, it is obviously sensible to prepare for leading the intercessions by praying for those who will be there, asking our God to lead us with his agenda in mind, rather than taking immediate charge ourselves. Then we have to give him a chance to answer! You may find that a quiet walk enables you to do this, or a time wandering round the empty church, or time spent on some of the mechanical jobs at home while you still your heart and resist the temptation to badger God with good ideas.

I have provided ideas to reflect the day's readings, and as you read through them you may well find that these ideas will spark off other thoughts of your own. Do use them however you wish – exactly as they stand, adapted to suit specific needs, or simply as a starting point. They are a resource to help you, not a cage to keep your own ideas out.

During the service be alert to what is being said and how God is moving among you, so that you can pick up on these threads, if it seems appropriate, during the intercessions. And if you have young children present, give some thought to how they can also be praying at this time. They might be following a picture prayer trail, singing a quiet worship song, drawing some situation they are praying for, or looking through the intercession pictures provided in children's communion books, such as *Jesus is Here* (Kevin Mayhew, 1993).

I have heard it said that since God can hear the prayers, it doesn't really matter if the congregation can't. I don't agree. In public worship it can be very distracting to be straining to hear, or isolating if you can hear only a vague mumble. Do take the trouble to practise speaking clearly and fairly slowly in the church, so that everyone can comfortably take in what you are saying. Bear in mind that nerves usually make us speed up somewhat, so speak extra slowly to allow for this.

Finally, don't recite what you have written, but pray it. Pray it both through the intentions and through the silences. Leading the intercessions carries a great responsibility, but it is also a great privilege.

SUSAN SAYERS

CONTENTS

LENT

EASTER

ORDINARY TIME

First Sunday
of Advent

*The gathered hopes of generations remind us to
get ourselves ready, so that Christ's return
will be a day of excitement and great joy.*

As we think about the fulfilment of all things today,
let us speak with the God of our making.

We pray that we will all be ready
to meet God face to face,
whenever and however that will be.

Silence

Lord, show us how to live:
and give us the courage to go forward.

We pray that all who lead and advise
may be led and advised by you,
so that our decisions are in line with your compassion.

Silence

Lord, show us how to live:
and give us the courage to go forward.

We pray that our families and neighbours
may be brought into contact
with the one true, living God
and know his affection for them.

Silence

Lord, show us how to live:
and give us the courage to go forward.

We pray that those hurt by injustice
may know your support,
and that the frail and timid
may know your encouragement and reassurance.

Silence

Lord, show us how to live:
and give us the courage to go forward.

We pray that those moving into eternity
through the gate of death
may be welcomed,
and their grieving loved ones comforted.

Silence

Lord, show us how to live:
and give us the courage to go forward.

We look with hope
to the fulfilment of all you have done,
and offer you our thanks and praise
for all your love.

Merciful Father,
**accept these prayers
for the sake of your Son,
our Saviour Jesus Christ. Amen.**

SECOND SUNDAY OF ADVENT

*It had been prophesied that there would be a
messenger to prepare the way for the coming of
the Messiah. Now John the Baptist appears
with his urgent message of repentance.*

We know that God is here with us,
and hears what is in our thoughts and in our hearts.

So we pray for all who claim to be Christians
all over the world.
We ask for a real longing for God in our lives;
a longing that is not satisfied by anything else.

Silence

Holy God:
we want to know you better.

We pray for the different countries
and those with power and influence.
We pray for honesty, justice and integrity.

Silence

Holy God:
we want to know you better.

We pray for those we love
and those we find it hard to relate to.
We pray for more love and forgiveness.

Silence

Holy God:
we want to know you better.

We pray for those in pain
and those imprisoned by addiction.
We pray for healing, wholeness and freedom.

Silence

Holy God:
we want to know you better.

We pray for those who have died
and now see you face to face.
We pray for those who miss them here.

Silence

Holy God:
we want to know you better.

We thank you for showing us
what needs putting right,
and for forgiving us all that is past.

Silence

Merciful Father,
**accept these prayers
for the sake of your Son,
our Saviour Jesus Christ. Amen.**

THIRD SUNDAY OF ADVENT

*Our period of preparation shifts from repentance
and forgiveness to the freed exhilaration of hope,
as the momentous truth of God's immanence
begins to dawn on us.*

God is here with us now.
Let us pray.

Father, we want to be ready to receive you.
Take us as we are and cultivate in us
a heart that longs for you and worships you
above and beyond everything else.

Silence

Come, O come:
Emmanuel, God with us.

We open to your love
the spiritual journeys of all who walk your way;
protect them from evil
and keep them steadfast in faith.

Silence

Come, O come:
Emmanuel, God with us.

We pray for those who give us support
and encourage us and listen to us
and make us laugh and share our sorrows.
Bless their lives and give them joy.

Silence

Come, O come:
Emmanuel, God with us.

We remember in God's presence
those whose memories are painful,
and those whose bitter resentment
cramps and distorts present relationships.
We ask for the healing only God can give.

Silence

Come, O come:
Emmanuel, God with us.

We call to mind those we know who have died,
and any who are close to death at the moment.
As they meet the one true God
open their hearts to receive his love,
mercy and forgiveness.

Silence

Come, O come:
Emmanuel, God with us.

We give God thanks
for the way none of us is beyond his saving love
and the way he has promised
to keep us ultimately safe.

Merciful Father,
**accept these prayers
for the sake of your Son,
our Saviour Jesus Christ. Amen.**

FOURTH SUNDAY OF ADVENT

*When we co-operate with God
amazing things happen.*

As we share in Mary and Elizabeth's joy
at the coming of our Saviour,
let us quieten and still ourselves
in the presence of God.

Heavenly Father, we can only marvel
at the way you are happy to work with us.
We want you to know
that we are willing to be used.

Silence

Let it be to me:
according to your will.

We call to mind before you
those whom we would love to know you
and we ask you to prepare their hearts
to recognise you.

Silence

Let it be to me:
according to your will.

We ask you to reassure and encourage us in this parish,
giving us insights to the real needs
and what you would have us do.

Silence

Let it be to me:
according to your will.

We ask you to give us courage
to continue working with you
even during the dark and dangerous times.

Silence

Let it be to me:
according to your will.

We call to mind those who are struggling
with poverty, illness or despair,
and ask you to comfort them,
using us however you want.

Silence

Let it be to me:
according to your will.

We remember those who have died
and thank you for the good
you have worked in their lives.
May we, with them, share in the life with you
that lasts for ever.

Silence

Let it be to me:
according to your will.

As we approach the festival of Christmas,
we praise and thank you for the full provision
you have given us
through the coming of Jesus.

Merciful Father,
**accept these prayers
for the sake of your Son,
our Saviour Jesus Christ. Amen.**

CHRISTMAS DAY

*Emmanuel – 'God with us' – is born at Bethlehem into
the human family. Now we will be able to understand,
in human terms, what God is really like.*

Emmanuel, God with us:
we welcome you!

As we celebrate God's coming to us
as a human child,
we bring the needs of our world
before the God we can trust.

We pray for all those who worship God
in every country of our world.
We pray for the grace
to know and love God more deeply.

Silence

Emmanuel, God with us:
we welcome you!

We pray for those who are spending this Christmas
apart from those they love.
We pray for those whose celebrations
are tempered with sorrow or fear.

Silence

Emmanuel, God with us:
we welcome you!

We pray for peace in the Holy Land
and for all who now live in the city of Bethlehem.

Silence

Emmanuel, God with us:
we welcome you!

We pray for those working over Christmas,
for all women giving birth
and all babies being born today.
We pray for their homes and families.

Silence

Emmanuel, God with us:
we welcome you!

We pray for those being born into eternal life
through the gate of death,
and commend them to God's love and mercy.

Silence

Emmanuel, God with us:
we welcome you!

Thank you, heavenly Father,
for the extraordinary love you show for us
in entering our world
through the natural channel of birth.

Merciful Father,
**accept these prayers
for the sake of your Son,
our Saviour Jesus Christ. Amen.**

First Sunday
of Christmas

*Jesus' perception and understanding of his purpose and
work begins to take shape throughout his childhood.*

Incarnate God:
we love you and we need you.

We have been called
to pray for one another in God's presence.
Let us settle ourselves to do that now.

We pray for all who are called to lead and teach
so that the truth of God's love
is shared throughout the world.
We ask for wisdom, energy
and sensitivity to God's prompting.

Silence

Incarnate God:
we love you and we need you.

We pray for all with power
and influence in our world.
We ask for a widespread desire
for those qualities of compassion and integrity.

Silence

Incarnate God:
we love you and we need you.

We pray for all parents and their children,
especially where there are conflicts,
anxious moments and gaps in communication.

Silence

Incarnate God:
we love you and we need you.

We pray for all missing persons and their families,
all who are rethinking their direction,
all who find life full of contradictions
at the moment.

Silence

Incarnate God:
we love you and we need you.

We pray for those who have come to the end
of their earthly life,
especially any who are unprepared.

Silence

Incarnate God:
we love you and we need you.

We give thanks and praise
for God's involvement in our lives.

Merciful Father,
**accept these prayers
for the sake of your Son,
our Saviour Jesus Christ. Amen.**

Second Sunday of Christmas

Christ is the way God tells people about himself.

We have met here
in the real presence of our God.
Let us pray to him now.

Silence

Though we cannot see you:
your love surrounds us.

We bring to mind the worldwide Christian Church,
both leaders and people,
as we begin another year.
We ask for a deeper awareness
of your presence among us.

Silence

Though we cannot see you:
your love surrounds us.

We bring to mind the troubled areas of our world
where corruption, injustice and violence
ruin lives and damage self worth.
We ask for your renewing and cleansing.

Silence

Though we cannot see you:
your love surrounds us.

We call to mind those we have spent time with
over this Christmas season;
the good and the disturbing conversations,
the joys and the aches of those we love.

Silence

Though we cannot see you:
your love surrounds us.

We bring to mind all who live away from home,
all refugees and all children in care.
We ask for the security that only you can give.

Silence

Though we cannot see you:
your love surrounds us.

We bring to mind those who have died recently
and all who grieve for them.
We ask for comfort to be given to the dying
and the assurance of your presence.

Silence

Though we cannot see you:
your love surrounds us.

We bring to mind the risks you were prepared to take
in becoming one of us out of love for us,
and we offer you our thanks and praise.

Merciful Father,
accept these prayers
for the sake of your Son,
our Saviour Jesus Christ. Amen.

THE EPIPHANY

Jesus, the hope of the nations,
is shown to the world.

We are all companions on a spiritual journey.
As we travel together, let us pray.

Silence

Light of the world:
shine in our darkness.

We pray that the worldwide Church
may always be ready
to travel in your way
and in your direction.

Silence

Light of the world:
shine in our darkness.

We pray for the nations
as they live through conflicts
and struggle with identity.
We long for all peoples
to acknowledge the true and living God.

Silence

Light of the world:
shine in our darkness.

We pray for the families and the streets we represent,
asking for a spirit of generous love,
understanding and mutual respect.

Silence

Light of the world:
shine in our darkness.

We pray for all who are finding their way
tedious, lonely or frightening at the moment;
for those who have lost their way
and do not know what to do for the best.

Silence

Light of the world:
shine in our darkness.

We pray for those who have come
to the end of their earthly journey,
and for those who have died unprepared.

Silence

Light of the world:
shine in our darkness.

We offer our thanks and praise
for the way you see us when we are still far off
and welcome us home.

Merciful Father,
accept these prayers
for the sake of your Son,
our Saviour Jesus Christ. Amen.

THE BAPTISM OF CHRIST
FIRST SUNDAY OF EPIPHANY

*Jesus is baptised, and God confirms
his identity and his calling.*

Let us pray to the God
who calls us each by name.

We pray for all baptised Christians
to live out their calling in loving and holy lives.
We pray for those preparing
for Baptism and Confirmation;
for parents and godparents
to be given the grace and perseverance
to keep faithfully the promises made.

Silence

Come, Holy Spirit:
fill our lives.

We pray for peace and integrity
in all our dealings as individuals,
and in local, national and international conflicts;
for openness to hear God's wisdom
and courage to follow his lead.

Silence

Come, Holy Spirit:
fill our lives.

We pray for harmony and understanding
in our relationships with family and neighbours;
for the willingness both to give and to receive,
for the generosity of forgiving love.

Silence

Come, Holy Spirit:
fill our lives.

We pray for those whose weariness or pain
makes it difficult for them to pray;
may they sense the support and love
of the Church of God.

Silence

Come, Holy Spirit:
fill our lives.

We pray for those whose souls
have left behind their frail and broken bodies
and can now fly freely to live in God's company
for the whole of eternity.
Bless and comfort their loved ones,
and bring us all in your good time,
to share the joy of heaven.

Silence

Come, Holy Spirit:
fill our lives.

We give you thanks for calling us by name
and keeping us safe
through all the storms and difficulties of this life,
in the power of the Holy Spirit.

Merciful Father,
accept these prayers
for the sake of your Son,
our Saviour Jesus Christ. Amen.

SECOND SUNDAY OF EPIPHANY

*As a marriage celebrates the beginning of a changed,
new life for the bride and groom, so our loving,
faithful God has chosen us and is ready to transform
our lives for the good of the world.*

Drawn by God's love and constant faithfulness to us,
let us pray.

We pray for all those who would love to believe
but cannot yet trust in the living God.
We pray for those who have rejected God
because of the unloving behaviour of his followers.

Silence

Fill us, Lord:
fill us to the brim.

We pray for all who give orders
and have influence over other people.
We pray that all peoples may be led justly
and with sensitivity.

Silence

Fill us, Lord:
fill us to the brim.

We pray for all our relationships
which need your transforming love;

we pray for those we irritate and upset
and those who have hurt and upset us.

Silence

Fill us, Lord:
fill us to the brim.

We pray for those whose lives feel empty
and lacking real meaning.
We pray for those whose frailty, pain or illness
makes it difficult to pray.

Silence

Fill us, Lord:
fill us to the brim.

We pray for those who are dying
and those who have completed their life on earth,
that they may be brought to peace and everlasting joy.

Silence

Fill us, Lord:
fill us to the brim.

We thank you for all the joys of loving relationships,
all the friendships we share,
and the love we are enabled to give.

Merciful Father,
**accept these prayers
for the sake of your Son,
our Saviour Jesus Christ. Amen.**

THIRD SUNDAY OF EPIPHANY

*The meaning of the scriptures
is revealed to the people.*

Let us still our bodies and our minds
as we pray together.

Silence

Open our ears, Lord:
and teach us to listen to you.

Lord God, as we call to mind
that we are members of the worldwide Church,
we pray for those who are insulted
or persecuted for our shared faith.
We stand alongside them now.

Silence

Open our ears, Lord:
and teach us to listen to you.

We pray that all of us
who inhabit planet Earth in this age
may learn to hear you again
and respond to your voice of love.

Silence

Open our ears, Lord:
and teach us to listen to you.

We pray that wherever materialism
or stress or sorrow or sin
have deafened us to your will,
we may be prompted to put things right.

Silence

Open our ears, Lord:
and teach us to listen to you.

We pray that our homes may be places
where you are welcomed and recognised
through the good and the troubled times.

Silence

Open our ears, Lord:
and teach us to listen to you.

We bring to your love all our fellow members
who are ill, injured or sad.
Alert us to see how we can help,
and give them a real sense
of your comforting presence.

Silence

Open our ears, Lord:
and teach us to listen to you.

We remember those who have travelled through life
and now have gone through death into eternity.
We thank you for their lives
and commend them to your keeping.
Prepare us all, through our living, for eternal life.

Silence

Open our ears, Lord:
and teach us to listen to you.

Thank you, Lord God, for all you have shown us
through Jesus, and through word and sacrament,
week by week.

Merciful Father,
accept these prayers
for the sake of your Son,
our Saviour Jesus Christ. Amen.

FOURTH SUNDAY OF EPIPHANY

*At eight days old, Jesus is presented in the temple,
and at the Purification is revealed to Simeon
and Anna as the promised Saviour who is
able to reveal to us our true selves.*

As we gather in Christ's name,
let us bring to mind those
who particularly need our prayer support.

We remember those who teach the faith
throughout the Church and throughout the world.
Keep them close to your guiding,
and open the hearts of those they teach
to hear and receive your truth.

Silence

Show us your ways:
and help us to walk in them.

We remember those in positions
of authority and influence
in this country and in all societies,
that needs may be noticed and addressed,
good values upheld and all people respected.

Silence

Show us your ways:
and help us to walk in them.

We remember those who looked after us
when we were very young,
and those who have no one to love and care for them.

We remember all young families
and all the children in our parish,
that they may be introduced to the one true God
and live their lives in his company.

Silence

Show us your ways:
and help us to walk in them.

We remember the elderly faithful
and especially those who are housebound
and can no longer join us to worship in person.
We thank you for their example
and ask you to increase our love for one another
across the age groups.

Silence

Show us your ways:
and help us to walk in them.

We remember those who have finished their lives on earth
and commit them to your everlasting care and protection.
We ask you to keep us faithful to the end of our life.

Silence

Show us your ways:
and help us to walk in them.

We remember with thankfulness
our elderly friends and relatives
and celebrate the way their lives
enrich our community.

Merciful Father,
accept these prayers
for the sake of your Son,
our Saviour Jesus Christ. Amen.

PROPER 1

Sunday between 3 and 9 February inclusive
(if earlier than the Second Sunday before Lent)

God calls his people and commissions them.

Let us pray together in the presence of our God.

We pray for all who have been called
to be workers in God's harvest,
searching for the lost and loving them into the kingdom.
We pray for those who teach God's love,
both by word and by the way they live.

Silence

Here I am, Lord:
ready for your service!

We pray for those in authority
and in positions of power,
that under their leadership
there may be mutual respect, integrity and justice.
We pray for discernment
to see where injustice needs righting
and when we need to speak out.

Silence

Here I am, Lord:
ready for your service!

We pray for families suffering poverty
or financial difficulties,
for families full of tension and disagreement,
and for families coping with grief or separation.

We pray for the extended families represented here.
We pray for better awareness
of how our behaviour affects others.

Silence

Here I am, Lord:
ready for your service!

We pray for those who have been working all night
and all who work long hours in poor conditions.
We pray for those who have no work and feel rejected.
We pray for any resisting what God is calling them into.

Silence

Here I am, Lord:
ready for your service!

We pray for those who have died
and those who grieve for the loss of their company.
We ask for the opportunity to prepare for death
by the way we live from now on.

Silence

Here I am, Lord:
ready for your service!

We thank you for the way you show us ourselves
and still accept us with love.

Merciful Father,
accept these prayers
for the sake of your Son,
our Saviour Jesus Christ. Amen.

PROPER 2

Sunday between 10 and 16 February inclusive
(if earlier than the Second Sunday before Lent)

The challenges and rewards of living by faith.

Knowing our need of God,
let us pray.

Father, we bring to mind our Church,
both here in *(name of town)* and throughout the world.
It is for right values and right priorities
that we pray, in all we decide and do.

Silence

Lord our God:
in you we put our trust.

We bring to mind all who lead and govern,
and all meetings where important decisions are made.
We pray that justice and mercy are upheld
in line with your loving will.

Silence

Lord our God:
in you we put our trust.

We bring to mind our circle of family and friends
with whom we share the good and the difficult times.
We pray for the grace to discern more readily
the good in each person and the gifts they have to offer.

Silence

Lord our God:
in you we put our trust.

We bring to mind those caught up
in the frenetic pressures of life,
and those who are stressed to breaking point.
We pray for insight and courage to change things.

Silence

Lord our God:
in you we put our trust.

We bring to mind the dying,
especially those who are alone,
and we remember those we know who have died.
May they and we share
in the everlasting joy of your presence.

Silence

Lord our God:
in you we put our trust.

We thank you, Father,
for all the wise teaching
you have given us through Christ.
Give us grace to be doers of the word
and not hearers only.

Merciful Father,
**accept these prayers
for the sake of your Son,
our Saviour Jesus Christ. Amen.**

Proper 3

Sunday between 17 and 23 February inclusive
(if earlier than the Second Sunday before Lent)

Jesus teaches us to love our enemies
and forgive those who sin against us.

God remembers our frailty;
let us pray to him now.

When conflicts threaten to disrupt our fellowship
in the church community,
deal with our frustrations and anger,
and give us the grace to forgive.

Silence

May we love one another:
as you have loved us.

When the luggage we carry from the past
interferes with our capacity to cope with the present,
heal the damage from our memories
and transform our experiences for good.

Silence

May we love one another:
as you have loved us.

When the differences in cultures
block our understanding of one another
and obstruct the peace process,
broaden our vision to discern the common ground.

Silence

May we love one another:
as you have loved us.

When the layers of resentment
have turned into rock,
dissolve them with the rain of your loving mercy.

Silence

May we love one another:
as you have loved us.

As those we have known and loved
pass through the gate of death,
have mercy on them,
and receive them into the joy
of your eternal kingdom.

Silence

May we love one another:
as you have loved us.

As we acknowledge the beauty
of loving even our enemies,
we thank you for the extraordinary love
you show us in Jesus.

Merciful Father,
accept these prayers
for the sake of your Son,
our Saviour Jesus Christ. Amen.

SECOND SUNDAY BEFORE LENT

*'He commands even the winds and
the water and they obey him.'*

Humankind has been brought into life by God.
We owe our very existence to him.
Let us pray to him now.

We pray for each living person
inhabiting our world with us,
with all the needs, emotions and experiences we share.
We pray that we may recognise one another
as brothers and sisters
sharing the same heavenly Father.

Silence

Lord of creation:
let your will be done.

We pray for greater reverence for God's creation
in the way we use and manage resources and wildlife.

Silence

Lord of creation:
let your will be done.

We pray for all of us in the ship of the Church,
that whenever storms rock the boat
and appear to threaten us,
we may trust God to bring us safely through.

Silence

Lord of creation:
let your will be done.

We pray for our children
and for all giving birth and being born today.
We long for the world they enter to be welcoming
and full of God's practical love.

Silence

Lord of creation:
let your will be done.

We pray for those who have chronic illness
and have to live in constant pain.
We ask for God's comfort
and reassurance to support them.

Silence

Lord of creation:
let your will be done.

We pray for those who have died,
thanking God for the example of lives well lived,
and for the total healing now received.

Merciful Father,
**accept these prayers
for the sake of your Son,
our Saviour Jesus Christ. Amen.**

SUNDAY BEFORE LENT

*God's glory makes Moses' face radiant, and it transfigures
Jesus as he prays on the mountain. Our lives, too, can
become increasingly radiant as the Spirit transforms us.*

As God's people,
let us pray to him now.

Father, we long to shine with your light.
Set our hearts on fire with love for you
and for one another.

Silence

May our lives proclaim:
that the Lord our God is holy.

Father, cleanse your Church of all hypocrisy,
and focus our attention on you,
so that divisions and barriers crumble to dust.

Silence

May our lives proclaim:
that the Lord our God is holy.

Father, send lives of light among the darkness
of injustice, corruption and despair,
and strengthen those who are already
shining in dark places all over the world.

Silence

May our lives proclaim:
that the Lord our God is holy.

Father, come into our homes
and make them places of welcome
where your love is woven into all our relationships.

Silence

May our lives proclaim:
that the Lord our God is holy.

Father, give courage to those
who have to suffer physical pain
or mental and emotional anguish.
Enable them to draw on your resources
and transform all our pain and sorrow.

Silence

May our lives proclaim:
that the Lord our God is holy.

Father, welcome into your kingdom of everlasting light
all who have come to the point of death.
Comfort those who miss their physical presence,
and bring us all to spend eternity
in the radiance of your presence.

Silence

May our lives proclaim:
that the Lord our God is holy.

Father, we thank you for the lives
of those who have directed us to you,
and for the way you never give up on us.

Merciful Father,
accept these prayers
for the sake of your Son,
our Saviour Jesus Christ. Amen.

First Sunday
of Lent

*Following his baptism, Jesus is severely tempted out in
the desert, and shows us how to overcome temptation.*

As children of our heavenly Father,
who knows us so well and loves us completely,
let us pray.

Father, knowing our weakness in the face of temptation,
we ask for your strength and protection
so that, though we stumble,
we shall not fall headlong.
Silence

Lead us not into temptation:
but deliver us from evil.

Father, we pray for all those who are fighting temptation
and finding it difficult to resist.
We ask you to help them see clearly,
and equip them with all they need
to choose what is right.
Silence

Lead us not into temptation:
but deliver us from evil.

Father, we pray for the Church
as it struggles to steer a straight course
true to your calling.
We pray for wisdom and courage,
honesty and the willingness to be vulnerable.
Silence

Lead us not into temptation:
but deliver us from evil.

Father, we pray for those we love,
whose company we enjoy.
We pray too for those who irritate us
and those whom we annoy.
Silence

Lead us not into temptation:
but deliver us from evil.

Father, we stand alongside all those who suffer,
all whose lives are in chaos or despair,
and all who live in the dark prison of guilt.
We pray for your reassurance and peace,
your understanding and compassion.
Silence

Lead us not into temptation:
but deliver us from evil.

We pray for the dying,
especially the unnoticed and despised.
We pray for those who have gone through death
and now see you face to face,
that they may receive your merciful forgiveness
and know the joy of living with you for ever.
Silence

Lead us not into temptation:
but deliver us from evil.

Father, we thank you for the knowledge
that nothing is beyond your forgiveness,
and no one beyond the limits of your love.
Silence

Merciful Father
accept these prayers
for the sake of your Son,
our Saviour Jesus Christ. Amen.

SECOND SUNDAY OF LENT

If only we will agree to put our faith in God,
he will fill our lives with meaning
and bring us safely to heaven.

Confident that God knows and loves each of us,
and understands our situation,
let us pray.

We pray for a deepening personal faith
in all Christians,
and renewed faith for all who are besieged by doubt.

Silence

You are our God:
in you we put our trust.

We pray that the Church
may be vigilant and courageous
in upholding the Christian faith,
and sensitive to the language and culture
of each person seeking for God in their lives.

Silence

You are our God:
in you we put our trust.

We long for a thirsting after God in our society;
for right living, justice and mercy
to be valued and worked for.

Silence

You are our God:
in you we put our trust.

We long for our homes and neighbourhoods
to reflect God's love
in our practical caring,
our hospitality and our parenting.

Silence

You are our God:
in you we put our trust.

We pray for those whose emotional pain
makes it difficult for them
to accept God's love and forgiveness;
and for all who feel that there is no hope.
We offer ourselves to be available
where you need us.

Silence

You are our God:
in you we put our trust.

We commend into your loving mercy the dying
and those who have made the journey through death.
With them we long to share the eternal joy
of your presence in heaven.

Silence

You are our God:
in you we put our trust.

We give you thanks and praise
for the endless love and patience you show us;
whenever we turn away,
please turn us back to you.

Merciful Father,
**accept these prayers
for the sake of your Son,
our Saviour Jesus Christ. Amen.**

THIRD SUNDAY
OF LENT

*We have God's invitation to come and drink freely
of his Spirit, but if we keep refusing his offer
it can eventually be withdrawn.*

As we thirst for God in our lives,
let us pray to him now.

Father, we thirst for your meaning
and your guidance
in all our work and worship and praise.
Fill us so full with your Spirit
that those we meet are drawn to meet you.

Silence

Living Spirit of God:
quench our thirst.

Father, in all the corruption and double standards
which damage and unnerve our world,
we thirst for your Spirit of truth, purity and goodness.

Silence

Living Spirit of God:
quench our thirst.

Father, we thirst for your Spirit of love
which notices needs,
considers no job beneath itself,
and delights in each person's gifts.

Silence

Living Spirit of God:
quench our thirst.

Father, we thirst for your Spirit of compassion
which binds up wounds,
supports the nervous and frail,
and visits the imprisoned and afraid.

Silence

Living Spirit of God:
quench our thirst.

Father, we thirst for your Spirit of life
as we call to mind those who have come
to the point of earthly death.
May they, and we in our turn,
find eternal refreshment and peace with you.

Silence

Living Spirit of God:
quench our thirst.

Father, may we thank you with our lives
as well as our lips
for the constant outpouring of your Spirit to us
throughout our lives.

Merciful Father,
**accept these prayers
for the sake of your Son,
our Saviour Jesus Christ. Amen.**

FOURTH SUNDAY OF LENT
MOTHERING SUNDAY

*While we are here in this life, given one another
to care for, we can learn the lessons of mutual
love and support and shared suffering.*

Gathered together as children in God's family, let us pray.

Lord, into our church community
pour the insight and discernment we need.
May we learn to love you more
as we learn to live and work in harmony,
focused on you and not on our divisions.

Silence

God our parent:
supply our needs.

Into the unease and weariness of our world
pour the reality and wholesome truth we need,
that we may learn mutual trust
and support one another in love.

Silence

God our parent:
supply our needs.

Lord, into the laughter and tears of family life
pour the freshness of your living presence,
as we work at our relationships
and deepen our love for one another.

Silence

God our parent:
supply our needs.

Lord, into the loneliness and pain
of those who feel rejected and unvalued
pour your compassion and reassurance,
that each person may know
the full extent of your love for them.

Silence

God our parent:
supply our needs.

Lord, may the dying know your reality
and find comfort and hope in you,
and may those who have died in faith
live for ever in the beauty of your holiness.

Silence

God our parent:
supply our needs.

Lord, may the way we live with one another
proclaim the truth of your constant love for us.

Merciful Father,
**accept these prayers
for the sake of your Son,
our Saviour Jesus Christ. Amen.**

FIFTH SUNDAY
OF LENT

When we are privileged to share in Christ's suffering,
we also share in his new life.

God is present with us now.
Let us bring him our prayers and concerns
for the Church and for the world.

Loving God, breathe your life into the Church,
so that we speak your love to the world
and are willing to suffer and prepared for sacrifice.

Silence

Lord, through your love:
transform our lives.

Loving God, breathe your peace into the world,
so that we work together co-operatively,
sensitive to one another's needs and differences.

Silence

Lord, through your love:
transform our lives.

Loving God, breathe your patience and forgiveness
into our homes and all our relationships,
so that we learn to cherish and respect one another
and act with generosity.

Silence

Lord, through your love:
transform our lives.

Loving God, breathe your encouragement
into every suffering and every sadness,
so that the dark and painful times
become places of strong spiritual growth.

Silence

Lord, through your love:
transform our lives.

Loving God, breathe your welcome
deep into the souls of the dying,
so that death is only the door
leading to the joy of eternal life with you.

Silence

Lord, through your love:
transform our lives.

Loving God, breathe your grace
into our knowing and our feeling,
so that we rejoice each step of the way,
whatever the terrain.

Merciful Father,
**accept these prayers
for the sake of your Son,
our Saviour Jesus Christ. Amen.**

PALM SUNDAY

*As Jesus rides into Jerusalem on a donkey, and the crowds
welcome him, we sense both the joy at the Messiah being
acclaimed, and the heaviness of his suffering which follows.
Jesus' mission is drawing to its fulfilment.*

As we recall Jesus entering Jerusalem,
let us gather our thoughts to pray.

Father, as the crowds welcomed Jesus
and sang your praises,
we pray that many more will welcome you
into their hearts and lives over the coming year.
We pray for opportunities to spread your good news
and courage to take them.

Silence

You are our God:
we welcome you!

Father, we recall the donkey Jesus rode on,
and we pray for that real humility in our hearts
which treats status and image casually,
and truth and loving service seriously.

Silence

You are our God:
we welcome you!

Father, the children sang and shouted your praise,
and we pray for the children in our homes,
our city and our land.
May we not fail them
in the support and teaching they need.

Silence

You are our God:
we welcome you!

Father, the crowds were responding
to the healing love they had seen in action in Jesus.
We bring to you in our love and imaginations now
all those we would have brought to Jesus
for healing and help.
Give them comfort and reassurance,
wholeness and hope.

Silence

You are our God:
we welcome you!

Father, Jesus knew he was riding to his death.
We pray for all on that last journey,
especially those burdened with fear and guilt.
We commend to your eternal love all who have died,
thanking you for the blessings we have received,
and even for the grief
which is part of the love we share.

Silence

You are our God:
we welcome you!

Father, we, too, spread our coats on the road
as we express our thankfulness
for all you have done for us
and the amazing extent of your love.

Merciful Father,
accept these prayers
for the sake of your Son,
our Saviour Jesus Christ. Amen.

Easter Day

*It is true. Jesus is alive for all time. The Lord of life
cannot be held by death. God's victory over sin
and death means that new life for us is a reality.*

With joy in our hearts,
come, let us pray together.

We remember with gratitude
the presence of the Church
in remote and highly populated areas
all over the world.
We pray for all other Christians rejoicing today
in the wonder of the Resurrection.

Silence

Life-giving God:
give us new life in you.

We pray that we may recognise you
as we walk through our days,
and we ask you to disturb any complacency
which is blurring our spiritual vision.

Silence

Life-giving God:
give us new life in you.

We pray for the courage to speak out
against injustice and oppression;
we pray that our leaders may establish and uphold
right values and sensitive legislation.

Silence

Life-giving God:
give us new life in you.

We pray that those of our families and friends
who have not yet met you
may be drawn into your company and introduced,
so that they can enjoy your faithfulness and love.

Silence

Life-giving God:
give us new life in you.

We remember those whose lives
are filled with pain, anxiety or sorrow,
and ask you to come alongside them
and speak their name.

Silence

Life-giving God:
give us new life in you.

With the words of Resurrection fresh in our minds,
we commend to your eternal love
those who have died,
that they may live with you for ever.

Silence

Life-giving God:
give us new life in you.

Father, may our lips and our lives
express our thanks and praise to you
for rescuing us and setting us free to live.

Merciful Father,
accept these prayers
for the sake of your Son,
our Saviour Jesus Christ. Amen.

SECOND SUNDAY OF EASTER

Having seen Jesus in person, the disciples are convinced
of the Resurrection. We too can meet him personally.

In the knowledge that God is here present with us,
let us pray.

Father, we thank you for the gifts of sight and insight,
and ask you to be there in all our looking.
Help us always to see with eyes of faith, love and honesty.

Silence

Open our eyes:
to see things your way, Lord.

We pray for our bishops, priests and deacons
in their demanding ministry of love,
that they may be given all the support,
grace and anointing they need.

Silence

Open our eyes:
to see things your way, Lord.

We pray for the gifts of discernment and integrity
among all those who govern, advise and lead.
Clear away all self-centred ambition
to free our leaders to serve.

Silence

Open our eyes:
to see things your way, Lord.

Whenever we have eye contact with family, friends,
neighbours or colleagues,
be there in that communication,
and remind us of our calling to love one another.

Silence

Open our eyes:
to see things your way, Lord.

We call to mind those whose eyes are wet with tears
or tense with pain.
Help them to sense your reassuring love
which can bring us through the darkest of valleys.

Silence

Open our eyes:
to see things your way, Lord.

Jesus is the firstfruit
of the new and eternal life we are promised in you.
We commend to your love
those who have recently walked through death
into that promise, and thank you for the privilege
of knowing them here on earth.

Silence

Open our eyes:
to see things your way, Lord.

Father we thank you for loving us
right through death into new life,
and we rejoice in your victory over evil.

Merciful Father,
accept these prayers
for the sake of your Son,
our Saviour Jesus Christ. Amen.

THIRD SUNDAY OF EASTER

*Those who know Jesus and recognise that he is the
anointed Saviour are commissioned to go out as his
witnesses to proclaim the good news.*

Let us gather with our prayers
before the God who knows each of us by name.

Father, we thank you that your Church
is made up of real people,
that it is a school for sinners,
and that you can work with us and through us
straight away.

Silence

Here I am, Lord:
send me!

Father, we pray for the newly baptised
and those who have recently returned to you;
help us, as your Church, to support them well
and delight in them as members together
of the body of Christ.

Silence

Here I am, Lord:
send me!

Father, we pray for your strength and protection
against all hypocrisy and double standards
in our society.
We pray for a spirit of genuine service
among all who lead and in all areas
where we have authority.

Silence

Here I am, Lord:
send me!

Father, we pray that you will make
our homes and our relationships
places where people know,
by the way we look at them and treat them,
that they are valued, cherished
and respected for who they are.

Silence

Here I am, Lord:
send me!

Father, as we call to mind all who have learned
to regard themselves with contempt,
draw near to them and whisper their true name
so that they discern the truth
of your love and respect for them.
And use our lives to affirm one another.

Silence

Here I am, Lord:
send me!

We pray for the dying
and those who have recently died,
commending them to the joy
and safe-keeping of your love.
We give thanks for all those who know and love us
and help us grow in faith.

Merciful Father,
**accept these prayers
for the sake of your Son,
our Saviour Jesus Christ. Amen.**

FOURTH SUNDAY OF EASTER

*Asked if he really is the Christ, Jesus directs his
questioners to look at his life in action and see for
themselves that he and the Father are one.*

As members together of the body of Christ,
let us pray to the true and living God.

We pray for the nurture
of each member of the Church;
for the newly baptised and for all
in ordained and lay ministry,
that our love for one another may show
as we work for the coming of the kingdom.
Silence
Direct our hearts, O Lord:
to love you more and more.

We pray for the gift of discernment,
so that we recognise God's presence,
and reverence his face
in the faces of those we meet.
Silence
Direct our hearts, O Lord:
to love you more and more.

We hold before you our monarchy
and all those who govern our country
and make its laws,
that we may act responsibly and with compassion,
attentive to real needs and good values.
Silence

Direct our hearts, O Lord:
to love you more and more.

We pray particularly for homes
filled with suspicion and envy,
and ask for the healing of old hurts,
together with hope and perseverance
as people set out on paths of reconciliation.
Silence
Direct our hearts, O Lord:
to love you more and more.

We pray for those whose capacity for trust and love
has been damaged by other people's sin.
We long for your healing
so that all who are imprisoned by their past
may walk freely into your future.
Silence
Direct our hearts, O Lord:
to love you more and more.

We pray for those who have recently passed through death,
that you will judge them with mercy,
so that, made whole in your love,
they may know the joy of your eternity.
Silence
Direct our hearts, O Lord:
to love you more and more.

We give you thanks and praise
for the salvation and restoration
that is now possible for us
through Christ's victory over death.

Merciful Father,
**accept these prayers
for the sake of your Son,
our Saviour Jesus Christ. Amen.**

FIFTH SUNDAY OF EASTER

Christ, breaking through the barrier of sin and death,
allows us to break into an entirely new way of living
which continues into eternity.

It is God's love that has drawn us here together.
Let us pray to him now.

Father, wherever Christians are fussing and arguing,
living outside your will
or without the responsible love you teach,
bring about deep cleansing, healing and renewing,
so that we can really be your body in our world.

Silence

Lord, you show us:
what loving really means.

Father, wherever injustice stifles human growth,
and selfish ambition distorts leadership,
bring about right and good government
throughout the world,
born of your wisdom and humility.

Silence

Lord, you show us:
what loving really means.

Father, as we watch our children growing,
remind us of our calling to grow more loving

in the ways we deal with conflict,
approach difficulties,
and address the needs of those we meet.

Silence

Lord, you show us:
what loving really means.

Father, in the places of long-term pain
and sudden shock,
of weariness, disappointment and fear,
bring about the peace which only you can give
and the comfort which speaks of hope.

Silence

Lord, you show us:
what loving really means.

Father, may the physical death of those we now recall
be nothing less than the gateway
to a new and lasting life in your love and protection.

Silence

Lord, you show us:
what loving really means.

So, heavenly Father,
we offer you our hearts
with all the love you find inside
and thank you for putting it there.

Merciful Father,
accept these prayers
for the sake of your Son,
our Saviour Jesus Christ. Amen.

SIXTH SUNDAY OF EASTER

*The continuing presence of God, as Holy Spirit,
leads us, as Jesus promised, into a personally
guided outreach to all nations.*

Drawn by the Holy Spirit,
we have arrived at this moment,
when we can pray together for the Church
and for the world.

Lord God, as members of your Church
in this generation,
we ask your guidance and blessing
for all our deacons, priests and bishops,
and all in training for lay and ordained ministry.
As the people of God, we ask for the gifts we need
for the work you need us to do.

Silence

You are with us:
every step of the way.

Lord God, this fragile, vulnerable planet
is so beautiful, and in such need of your guidance;
we pray for a deeper valuing
of our universe and of one another;
for your kingdom to come on earth as in heaven.

Silence

You are with us:
every step of the way.

Lord God, may our homes be centres of love,
acceptance and welcome;

we pray that you will make your home among us
in each room and each relationship.

Silence

You are with us:
every step of the way.

Lord God, we pray for all who are weighed down
with doubts, fears and misgivings;
all who are haunted by the past
or scared by the future.
We ask for them awareness of your constant presence
and courage to place their hand in yours.

Silence

You are with us:
every step of the way.

Lord God, as we remember those
whose earthly life has come to an end,
we pray that they, and we in our turn,
may recognise you in heaven
and live in your light for ever.

Silence

You are with us:
every step of the way.

Lord God, we give you thanks
for all the blessings you shower on us
along the way of life,
and for the painstaking guidance you provide.

Merciful Father,
accept these prayers
for the sake of your Son,
our Saviour Jesus Christ. Amen.

ASCENSION DAY

Having bought back our freedom with the giving of his life, Jesus enters into the full glory to which he is entitled.

As we celebrate together, let us pray together.

God of love, as we celebrate this festival
of Jesus' entry into heaven as Saviour and Lord,
we pray for unity in the Church
and reconciliation and renewed vision.

Silence

Both heaven and earth:
are full of God's glory.

As we recall the shout of praise in heaven
as the Lamb of God appears,
we pray for all who are hailed as heroes
and given great honour on earth;
for all who worship anyone or anything
other than the true God.

Silence

Both heaven and earth:
are full of God's glory.

We pray for all farewells and homecomings
among our families and in our community,
and for all who have lost touch with loved ones
and long for reunion.

Silence

Both heaven and earth:
are full of God's glory.

We pray for those who are full of tears,
and cannot imagine being happy again;
we pray for the hardened and callous,
whose inner hurts have never yet been healed.
We pray for wholeness and comfort and new life.

Silence

Both heaven and earth:
are full of God's glory.

We commend to your eternal love
those we remember who have died,
and we pray too for those
who miss their physical presence.

Silence

Both heaven and earth:
are full of God's glory.

We praise and bless you, God of our making,
for the way you draw us deeper
into the meaning of life.

Merciful Father,
accept these prayers
for the sake of your Son,
our Saviour Jesus Christ. Amen.

SEVENTH SUNDAY OF EASTER

*Jesus lives for all time in glory; we can live the fullness
of Resurrection life straight away.*

Let us pray to the God who gives us so much
and loves us so completely.

We pray for a fresh outpouring of your Spirit
in all areas of the Church,
till our lives are so changed for good
that people notice and are drawn
to seek you for themselves.

Silence

We are your people:
and you are our God.

We pray for godly leaders and advisers
all over the world,
and for the courage to speak out
against injustice and evil.

Silence

We are your people:
and you are our God.

We pray for those affected
by our behaviour and our conversation,
that we may in future
encourage one another by all we say and do.

Silence

We are your people:
and you are our God.

We pray for those as yet unborn,
that the good news will reach them too;
we pray for those who have rejected God
because of the behaviour of his followers;
we pray for all who have lost their way.

Silence

We are your people:
and you are our God.

We pray for the dying,
especially those who are unprepared or frightened.
Welcome into your kingdom
those who have died in faith;
may they live with you for ever.

Silence

We are your people:
and you are our God.

Thank you, Lord, for the new life
you have enabled us to live.

Merciful Father,
accept these prayers
for the sake of your Son,
our Saviour Jesus Christ. Amen.

PENTECOST

*As Jesus promised, the Holy Spirit is poured out
on the apostles and the Church is born.*

As the Spirit enables us,
let us gather ourselves to pray.

May all Church leaders,
ordained ministers and the laity
be filled to overflowing
with love for your people,
and kindled with fresh zeal
for spreading the good news of the Gospel.

Silence

Spirit of the living God:
fall afresh on us.

May all those negotiating for peace
in the delicate areas of national conflict,
industrial disputes and entrenched bitterness,
be blessed with the peace of God,
tranquil and patient beneath the pressures.

Silence

Spirit of the living God:
fall afresh on us.

In our homes and places of work,
our schools and hospitals,
may there always be time
for the warmth of loving concern
and the comfort of being valued.

Silence

Spirit of the living God:
fall afresh on us.

Give help to all rescue workers and keep them safe;
may all who are trapped in damaged bodies or minds,
in poverty or tyranny, in earthquakes, floods or storms,
be brought to freedom and safety
and be aware of your love for them.

Silence

Spirit of the living God:
fall afresh on us.

We pray for those who have died
and all who mourn their going;
calm the fears of the dying
and have mercy on us all.

Silence

Spirit of the living God:
fall afresh on us.

We thank you, heavenly Father,
for the gift of your Holy Spirit among us;
and we look forward to the future
infused with your life.

Merciful Father,
**accept these prayers
for the sake of your Son,
our Saviour Jesus Christ. Amen.**

TRINITY SUNDAY

The unique nature of God is celebrated today,
as we reflect on the truth that God is Creator,
Redeemer and Life-giver.

Let us pray to the Father,
in the power of the Holy Spirit,
through Jesus, the Son.

We pray for all theologians
and those who teach the faith
in colleges and Bible study groups
throughout the Church.
We pray for Godly wisdom and human insight.

Silence

Holy God:
help us to know you more.

We pray for peace and co-operation,
harmony and mutual respect
in all our dealings with one another
locally, nationally and internationally.

Silence

Holy God:
help us to know you more.

We pray for those who depend on us,
and those on whom we depend,
for our physical and spiritual needs.

Enable us to honour one another
as children of your making.
Silence

Holy God:
help us to know you more.

We pray for those who feel fragmented;
and for those forced to live apart from loved ones
through war, political unrest,
natural disasters or poverty.
We commend their pain to your comforting.

Silence

Holy God:
help us to know you more.

We remember those who told us of you
through their words and lives;
we think of those who have died in faith
and ask that we may share with them
in the joy of your presence for ever.

Silence

Holy God:
help us to know you more.

We give you thanks for meeting us where we are,
and travelling with us in person.

Merciful Father,
**accept these prayers
for the sake of your Son,
our Saviour Jesus Christ. Amen.**

PROPER 4

*Sunday between 29 May and 4 June inclusive
(if after Trinity Sunday)*

*The good news we have been given is not just for us,
but to pass on to the rest of the world.*

We have gathered here today
in the company of the true God.
Let us pray to him now.

Lord, we ask for your blessing and anointing
on all involved with mission and outreach,
both here and abroad, among children and adults,
as they commit themselves
to spreading the good news.

Silence

You are the living God:
let your will be done in us.

We pray for all who have influence and authority,
through their political standing, fame or wealth;
speak into their hearts of righteousness and justice,
integrity and compassion.

Silence

You are the living God:
let your will be done in us.

We pray that we may take seriously
our responsibilities for nurturing our children
and those who do not yet know God's love.
Transform our living to reveal that love.

Silence

You are the living God:
let your will be done in us.

Lord, we call to mind those in need
of comfort and reassurance,
all in pain and mental anguish.
We pray for the lapsed and the doubting
and those who need your good news this week.

Silence

You are the living God:
let your will be done in us.

Have mercy on those who have recently died
and those on that last journey now.
Bring us all safely to heaven
to live with you for ever.

Silence

You are the living God:
let your will be done in us.

Lord, we thank you for the good news we have received;
may we be ready to share our joy with others.

Merciful Father,
accept these prayers
for the sake of your Son,
our Saviour Jesus Christ. Amen.

PROPER 5

Sunday between 5 and 11 June inclusive
(if after Trinity Sunday)

Our God is full of compassion; he hears our crying
and it is his nature to rescue us.

Let us bring to the God who loves us
our prayers and concerns for the Church and the world.

God of compassion,
take our hearts of stone
and give us feeling hearts,
so that we as the Church
may be more responsive
to the needs and sorrows around us.

Silence

God of love:
show us the Way.

God of wisdom,
teach all in authority,
inspire those who lead,
protect each nation from evil,
and further each right decision.

Silence

God of love:
show us the Way.

God of tenderness,
dwell in our homes
through all the times of joy

and all the heartaches and sadness,
teaching us to show one another
the love you show to us.

Silence

God of love:
show us the Way.

God of wholeness,
speak into the despair and loneliness
of all who struggle with life and its troubles;
reassure, affirm and encourage them,
and alert us to ways we can help.

Silence

God of love:
show us the Way.

God of peace,
be with the dying,
and as you welcome those who have died in faith
into the full life of your kingdom,
we, too, remember them with thanks and love.

Merciful Father,
**accept these prayers
for the sake of your Son,
our Saviour Jesus Christ. Amen.**

Proper 6

Sunday between 12 and 18 June inclusive
(if after Trinity Sunday)

God has the authority and the desire to forgive our sins
completely and set us free from guilt.

Knowing your love for us, Holy God,
we have come before you to pray together.

We pray for all who have the care of souls,
and are entrusted with helping others to repentance
and giving them good counsel.
We pray for those called to speak God's values,
whatever the danger and regardless of popularity.

Silence

Work in us, Lord:
work in us for good.

We pray for those who refuse
to allow injustice or evil to go unchallenged;
for all who are under pressure
to behave wrongly
or keep quiet about something they know to be wrong.

Silence

Work in us, Lord:
work in us for good.

We pray for more loving forgiveness
in all our relationships,
for more self-knowledge,

the grace to recognise where we are in the wrong,
and the courage to seek God's forgiveness.

Silence

Work in us, Lord:
work in us for good.

We pray for all imprisoned by guilt, resentment,
bitterness and self-pity,
that they may come to know the relief of being forgiven.
We pray for all innocent victims,
that their scars may be completely healed.

Silence

Work in us, Lord:
work in us for good.

We pray for those who have died
unprepared to meet you,
and for all who have died in faith.
Have mercy on us all.

Silence

Work in us, Lord:
work in us for good.

Thank you, Lord God,
for the wideness of your mercy
and the completeness of your forgiveness,
which restores us to you in such joy.

Merciful Father,
**accept these prayers
for the sake of your Son,
our Saviour Jesus Christ. Amen.**

PROPER 7

Sunday between 19 and 25 June inclusive
(if after Trinity Sunday)

God is close through all our troubles,
and can bring us safely through them.

Let us pray to the faithful God who knows us already,
and loves us so much.

We pray that any barriers within the Church,
built up by fear or prejudice, misunderstanding or hurt,
may be broken down in Christ and unity restored.

Silence

Whatever our journey, O Lord:
walk with us on the way.

We pray for our world to be governed wisely and well,
with proper consideration
for the vulnerable and weak,
with co-operation, honesty and respect for all.

Silence

Whatever our journey, O Lord:
walk with us on the way.

We pray for the healing
of hurts and tensions in our families;
and for our friends,
thanking you for the blessings they give;
as friends of Christ, may we be
generous in our friendships.

Silence

Whatever our journey, O Lord:
walk with us on the way.

We pray for those disturbed by mental illness,
and for all who are rejected and despised.
We pray for all in desolate situations at the moment,
and ask for your comfort and healing.

Silence

Whatever our journey, O Lord:
walk with us on the way.

We remember those whose earthly life has ended,
and for those grieving for loved ones.
Enfold them in your love
and let them become aware of you beside them.

Silence

Whatever our journey, O Lord:
walk with us on the way.

We give you thanks, O Lord,
for the loving way you provide for us,
even during the darkest times.

Merciful Father,
accept these prayers
for the sake of your Son,
our Saviour Jesus Christ. Amen.

PROPER 8

Sunday between 26 June and 2 July inclusive

When we are called to follow Jesus, that means
total commitment, with no half-measures.

Holy God, you have called us
to meet and pray together,
and here we are.

We pray for those called
to lay and ordained ministry in your Church,
and for those at present testing their vocation.
We lay before you the work that needs doing here
and ask you to provide people to do it.

Silence

We ask in Jesus' name:
give us grace to discern your answer.

We pray for those called to serve you
in positions of authority and influence;
for all leaders to see true greatness as service
and true strength as humility.

Silence

We ask in Jesus' name:
give us grace to discern your answer.

We pray for those called to marriage,
and those called to the single life,
for parents and grandparents,
sons and daughters,

for acceptance of what we cannot change
and strength to live the Christian life
in our present situation.

Silence

We ask in Jesus' name:
give us grace to discern your answer.

We pray for those whose lives
are full of disappointment, disillusion and discontent;
for all who struggle with great perseverance
in difficult circumstances.
We pray for your strength, encouragement and direction.

Silence

We ask in Jesus' name:
give us grace to discern your answer.

We pray for those called, through death, into eternal life
and freedom from all their pain and suffering.
Receive them with mercy
and welcome them into your kingdom.

Silence

We ask in Jesus' name:
give us grace to discern your answer.

We thank you, Holy God, for your promise
that where two or three are gathered in your name
you will grant their requests.

Merciful Father,
accept these prayers
for the sake of your Son,
our Saviour Jesus Christ. Amen.

PROPER 9

Sunday between 3 and 9 July inclusive

In Christ we become a new creation.

Let us bring our cares and concerns
before the God who loves us.
We pray for more workers
to gather in the harvest of the kingdom;
for our churches to be places of welcome
and wholesome spiritual nurture;
for a healthy balance of tradition and exploration.

Silence

Use us, Lord:
in the building of your kingdom.

We pray for our nation and the nations of the world;
for an upholding of godly principles and just laws,
for reconciliation, peace and mutual co-operation.

Silence

Use us, Lord:
in the building of your kingdom.

We pray for those among our families and friends
who have no idea of the new life you offer;
we pray for them to discover you
so they may share the joy of living in your love.

Silence

Use us, Lord:
in the building of your kingdom.

We pray for those suffering from leprosy
and other skin disorders,
for those disfigured by disease or accidents,
for the lonely, the confused and the outcasts.

Silence

Use us, Lord:
in the building of your kingdom.

We pray for the dying, and their loved ones,
for those who have passed through death,
and the families and friends who miss them.
Surround them with your love.

Silence

Use us, Lord:
in the building of your kingdom.

We praise you, Lord, and give you thanks
for the fullness of this new life
you have given us in Christ;
keep us renewed and filled with your Spirit.

Merciful Father,
accept these prayers
for the sake of your Son,
our Saviour Jesus Christ. Amen.

PROPER 10

Sunday between 10 and 16 July inclusive

*Straighten your lives out
and live by God's standards of love.*

Let us pray to God,
knowing we can trust him.

We pray that as Christians we may take to heart
the need to walk the talk,
and live out what we profess.
We pray that nothing may get so important to us
that it pushes God's values aside.

Silence

Father:
let only your will be done.

We pray that those in authority and power
do not lose touch with the needs of those they serve,
so that the poor and oppressed and vulnerable
are always given value and respect.

Silence

Father:
let only your will be done.

We pray for those in our families
whom we love and have hurt or upset;
we pray too for those who have hurt or upset us,
and ask for God's reconciliation and healing.

Silence

Father:
let only your will be done.

We pray for those who have lost hope
of being rescued, noticed or valued;
for the complacent who cannot see their poverty,
for the prejudiced who mistake blindness for sight.

Silence

Father:
let only your will be done.

We pray for our loved ones
who have reached the moment of death,
and thank you for the example of their lives.
We commend them all to your safe keeping.

Silence

Father:
let only your will be done.

We give you thanks, Lord God, for the hope
and encouragement you give us
on our journey of faith.

Merciful Father,
**accept these prayers
for the sake of your Son,
our Saviour Jesus Christ. Amen.**

PROPER 11

Sunday between 17 and 23 July inclusive

*Against impossible odds
God has reconciled us to himself, in Christ.*

Our God is always ready to listen.
Let us pray to him now.

Father, continue to pour out your gifts on the Church,
so that many may be saved
and our faith may grow strong
and bear much fruit.

Silence

God of Love:
we put our trust in you.

Look with mercy on the conflicts of our world;
realign our values and goals
until they are in line with your will,
and our laws and expectations reflect your justice and love.

Silence

God of Love:
we put our trust in you.

Bless our homes and families
and all our neighbours and friends;
train us to listen to one another with full attention,
and recognise one another's gifts.

Silence

God of Love:
we put our trust in you.

Encourage the hesitant, curb the overpowering,
heal the sick, refresh the exhausted,
soften the hardened hearts,
open the eyes of the complacent,
and comfort all who are sad.

Silence

God of Love:
we put our trust in you.

Welcome into your eternity
all those who have died in faith;
may we in our turn share with them
the joy of living with you for ever.

Silence

God of Love:
we put our trust in you.

Thank you, Lord our God,
for the hope you have given us through Christ,
which enables us to enjoy living in eternity
even while we still journey here.

Merciful Father,
**accept these prayers
for the sake of your Son,
our Saviour Jesus Christ. Amen.**

PROPER 12

Sunday between 24 and 30 July inclusive

*Keep asking for God's Spirit and he will
keep pouring out his blessing on you.*

Heavenly Father, as you have taught us, through Jesus,
we come to you in prayer.

We pray for all who uphold and teach the faith,
for young Christians in schools and universities,
for Christians witnessing to their faith at work,
for all in danger of persecution.
We pray for your strength and courage.

Silence

In all things, Father:
let your will be done.

We pray for discernment and wisdom
as we strive for international co-operation
in managing the world's resources;
for perseverance as we work
towards peace and reconciliation.

Silence

In all things, Father:
let your will be done.

We pray for the good sense
in our family and community life
that knows the difference
between generosity and indulgence,
between lenience and neglect of responsibility.

Silence

In all things, Father:
let your will be done.

We pray for all victims of abuse and tyranny,
for all who suffer long-term effects
of torture, war or disease;
we pray for the grace to forgive,
and for healing of body, mind and spirit.

Silence

In all things, Father:
let your will be done.

We pray for those who have died,
and particularly for those
who have no one to mourn their going;
for those who have died unnoticed.
We pray that they may rest in your peace for ever.

Silence

In all things, Father:
let your will be done.

Father, we thank you for all the gifts
you pour out to us each day of our lives;
keep us asking, and keep us seeking you.

Merciful Father,
accept these prayers
for the sake of your Son,
our Saviour Jesus Christ. Amen.

PROPER 13

Sunday between 31 July and 6 August inclusive

True richness is not material wealth;
true security is not a financial matter.

Let us pray to God our Father,
knowing that we are all precious to him.

Father, we thank you for all those
who give to support the work of the Church;
bless our giving, guide our spending,
and help us to value the true wealth
of your abundant love.

Silence

The Lord is our shepherd:
there is nothing we shall want.

We pray for the world's economy;
for fair management and distribution of resources;
for fair trade and just wages;
for greater awareness and concern about injustice;
for a commitment to our responsibilities
as planet-sharers and earth-dwellers.

Silence

The Lord is our shepherd:
there is nothing we shall want.

We pray for all parents with young children,
thanking you for them
and asking you to bless and guide their parenting;
we pray for families in debt;

for those whose homes have been repossessed,
and those whose financial security
makes them forgetful of your love.

Silence

The Lord is our shepherd:
there is nothing we shall want.

We pray for those who are burdened
with financial worries
and all who struggle to make ends meet,
all over the world;
we pray for the emotionally and spiritually bankrupt,
and those who do not yet know God's love for them.

Silence

The Lord is our shepherd:
there is nothing we shall want.

We pray for those who have died,
and those on that last journey at this moment;
for a merciful judgement
and the everlasting joy of heaven.

Silence

The Lord is our shepherd:
there is nothing we shall want.

Father, we give you thanks
for the extraordinary generosity of your love for us,
which lasts beyond death into the whole of eternity.

Merciful Father,
accept these prayers
for the sake of your Son,
our Saviour Jesus Christ. Amen.

PROPER 14

Sunday between 7 and 13 August inclusive

Have faith in God, and get yourself ready to meet him.

As God's beloved children,
let us come to him and open our hearts to him.

Father, you know both our gifts as a congregation
and the needs of those in this parish,
and we ask you to bless our ministry in this place.
Strengthen and encourage all Church leaders
and deepen our faith and sure hope.

Silence

Lord our God:
we believe and trust in you.

Father, heal our nation and all the nations
of what is in the past and still corrodes the present,
so that we may build on good foundations
and learn to govern ourselves with honesty,
respect for one another and sensitivity to needs.

Silence

Lord our God:
we believe and trust in you.

Father, be present in the daily living
of our homes and in all our relationships;
make us more trustworthy in our friendships,
and strengthen our resolve to live our faith in action.

Silence

Lord our God:
we believe and trust in you.

We call to mind all whose capacity to trust
has been damaged;
for those who are victims of injustice or corruption;
for the very young and the very old,
the frail, the vulnerable and the bereaved.

Silence

Lord our God:
we believe and trust in you.

We remember those
who have completed their earthly life in faith
and have now seen you face to face.
May they know the peace of eternity;
we too look forward to sharing that life of joy.

Silence

Lord our God:
we believe and trust in you.

Thank you, Lord our God,
for the glorious hope you have set before us.

Merciful Father,
accept these prayers
for the sake of your Son,
our Saviour Jesus Christ. Amen.

PROPER 15

Sunday between 14 and 20 August inclusive

*When we fix our eyes on Jesus
our lives will reflect his nature.*

God is close to us as we pray.
He is attentive to us now.

Lord, whenever you weep over our harshness,
may your tears melt our hearts of stone.
Whenever you grieve over our double standards,
shock us into honesty again.
Make us receptive to your teaching,
willing to take your risks
and eager to run with our eyes fixed on Jesus.
Silence

Lead us, Lord:
to walk in your ways.

Whenever the news overwhelms us,
nudge us to fervent prayer.
Wherever leaders meet to negotiate peace,
be present at the conference table.
Breathe your values into our thinking,
tear down the divisive barriers
and renew us to lead the world into loving.
Silence

Lead us, Lord:
to walk in your ways.

Whenever tempers are frayed
and patience is wearing thin,
give us space to collect ourselves and try again.
Whenever the demands of family and friends
remind us of our limitations,

minister graciously through our weakness
and teach us the humility of apologising.

Silence

Lead us, Lord:
to walk in your ways.

Whenever people are enveloped by pain
or desolate grief or total exhaustion,
bring refreshment and peace, tranquillity and hope.
Wherever the grip of the past
prevents free movement into the future,
bring release and healing.

Silence

Lead us, Lord:
to walk in your ways.

Whenever the dying are fearful and distressed,
give comfort and reassurance on that last journey.
Bless those who care for them
and those who mourn their going.
In mercy receive the dead
into the life of your heaven,
and prepare us, through our lives now, for eternity.

Silence

Lead us, Lord:
to walk in your ways.

Holy God, we love the beauty and goodness
of your nature,
and thank you for the gift of your Spirit
to guide us to walk in your ways.

Merciful Father,
**accept these prayers
for the sake of your Son,
our Saviour Jesus Christ. Amen.**

PROPER 16

Sunday between 21 and 27 August inclusive

*God sets his leaders apart to challenge prejudices and
assumptions, and alert people to the truth.*

Let us pray to the God who has loved us
throughout our whole life.

Lord our God, broaden our vision of your nature
and help us respond to your calling,
whether it suits us or not,
and whether it is convenient or not.

Silence

Lord God:
you are our hope.

May the whole Church reflect your light and beauty
in the love for God and neighbour,
displayed in corporate worship
and individual godly living.

Silence

Lord God:
you are our hope.

May no corruption, cruelty or injustice go unchallenged
in any part of our world,
however unpopular the challenging may be.
May our society protect the vulnerable
and encourage mutual care and support.

Silence

Lord God:
you are our hope.

May our care of the very young and the elderly
imitate the faithful and generous caring of our God;
may we overcome our envies, jealousies and grievances,
so that in God's love we can look at one another face to face,
and practise the liberating work of forgiveness.

Silence

Lord God:
you are our hope.

May all whose bodies cause them pain or immobility
be affirmed in value by loving encounter
with Jesus and his followers;
and may those who are spiritually crippled
be set free to love and serve God.

Silence

Lord God:
you are our hope.

May those who have died in faith
live for ever in the joy and peace of heaven
as children of Promise;
and may those who miss their company
be comforted and supported.

Silence

Lord God:
you are our hope.

May our gratitude to the One who sets us free
be shown each day in the way we live and speak.

Merciful Father
accept these prayers
for the sake of your Son,
our Saviour Jesus Christ. Amen.

PROPER 17

Sunday between 28 August and 3 September inclusive

*When we live God's way, both individually and as
a community, we will be greatly blessed.*

Let us do the work of prayer that God has asked of us.

As the body constantly breathes,
may the Church, the body of Christ,
constantly pray,
breathing God's life into all its members and activities.

Silence

The Lord is our helper:
we shall not be afraid.

As a new week begins in our world,
may wrong priorities be challenged and adjusted,
may our societies reflect God's concern
for righteousness, true justice and responsive love,
and may all leaders grow in humility,
attentive to the needs of those they serve.

Silence

The Lord is our helper:
we shall not be afraid.

As we call to mind our loved ones,
all who depend on us,
and those on whom we depend,
all with whom we laugh, cry, work or play,
cleanse and refresh our relationships
and give us greater love, understanding and forgiveness.

Silence

The Lord is our helper:
we shall not be afraid.

We think of those who are in prison,
locked in cells or depression or dysfunctional bodies;
we think of those in hospital wards and accident centres,
those unable to reach medical help
and those on long waiting-lists for operations;
as we think of them all, we pray for them all.

Silence

The Lord is our helper:
we shall not be afraid.

We remember the dying and those who love them;
we remember those whose earthly life has come to an end,
and we commend them to God's undying love.

Silence

The Lord is our helper:
we shall not be afraid.

With love in our hearts
for God our Maker and Redeemer,
we choose to walk in his ways
through this day and all our days.

Merciful Father,
accept these prayers
for the sake of your Son,
our Saviour Jesus Christ. Amen.

PROPER 18

Sunday between 4 and 10 September inclusive

*Following Jesus is expensive –
it costs everything, but it's worth it.*

Let us pray to the God who has watched our growing
throughout our lives, and loves us.

Lord, there is nothing hidden from you.
All our thoughts and plans and secret fears
are open to you, even when we try to hide them.
Deal with the doubts and misgivings
and fears of your Church,
with the love and mercy which are part of your nature.

Silence

Gracious God:
in you we can trust.

Lord, you feel for the oppressed and the forgotten;
you understand the damage which can lead to violence,
the insecurity which can lead to defensiveness,
and the neglect which can lead to lack of control.
Heal the nations; restore what has been lost;
and turn our hearts to discern your will.

Silence

Gracious God:
in you we can trust.

Lord, you see the point at which
discussions turn to arguments
and preferences to selfishness.
You know the love inside our hearts for one another
that sings and dances and aches and worries.

Work on us now in the depth of our being
and bless our loved ones with a sense of joy.

Silence

Gracious God:
in you we can trust.

Lord, you suffer with those who suffer
and weep with those who weep;
we, too, stand alongside them now
in whatever pain, distress or sorrow
is engulfing them,
longing for them to be comforted.

Silence

Gracious God:
in you we can trust.

Lord, your death and resurrection
proclaim the message of hope
amongst the tears of our grieving
for those who have died.
Welcome them into the eternal light of your kingdom.

Silence

Gracious God:
in you we can trust.

Lord, your way may be costly
but to whom else could we go?
For you alone have the words of eternal life,
and we offer you ourselves.

Merciful Father,
accept these prayers
for the sake of your Son,
our Saviour Jesus Christ. Amen.

Proper 19

Sunday between 11 and 17 September inclusive

*Jesus does not avoid the company
of sinners but befriends them.*

Let us pray to the God who longs for all to be rescued.

Heavenly Father, thank you for our bishops,
priests and deacons, and all who are called
to the different ministries in the Church.
Bless them as they work in your service
and uphold them with your power.

Silence

God our shepherd:
all our needs are known to you.

Thank you for all peace initiatives
and every genuine attempt at negotiation
in conflict resolution.
May those who govern be governed by your love;
may those who lead be led by your directing;
may the whole world come to know its need of you.

Silence

God our shepherd:
all our needs are known to you.

Thank you, Lord God, for our families and friends,
those we meet each day and those we seldom see;
draw all our loved ones closer to you,
and search out those whose faith
is fragile or fragmented.

Silence

God our shepherd:
all our needs are known to you.

Heavenly Father, as we recall the needs
of those who are sad or lonely,
lost, or afraid of what they have become,
we pray for the knowledge of your love
to wrap warmly around them,
and your living presence
to bring them to a place of safety and hope.

Silence

God our shepherd:
all our needs are known to you.

Have mercy, Lord God,
on those who have recently died;
may they enjoy the eternal life of heaven,
where there is no more pain, sorrow or weariness,
and every tear shall be wiped away.

Silence

God our shepherd:
all our needs are known to you.

Thank you, heavenly Father,
for your long-suffering patience with us.

Merciful Father,
accept these prayers
for the sake of your Son,
our Saviour Jesus Christ. Amen.

PROPER 20

Sunday between 18 and 24 September inclusive

*If you cannot be trusted with worldly riches,
or even small amounts of money, then you will
not be trusted with spiritual riches either.*

As God has taught us, let us pray
for the coming of the kingdom in every situation.

We long for the Church to be pure and holy,
alight with God's love and compassion,
and free from behaviour which is unworthy
of God's chosen people.

Silence

God our Father:
let your kingdom come.

We long for the nations to be wisely governed,
with just laws and a sense of vision
which reflects the best of human nature.
We long for peace and mutual respect
in each community throughout the world.

Silence

God our Father:
let your kingdom come.

We long for our homes to be filled with God's love,
so we are happy to put ourselves out for others,
to listen with full attention, and to value one another.

We long to clear away anything in our life-style
which competes with God for our commitment.

Silence

God our Father:
let your kingdom come.

We long for those who feel neglected
or rejected by society
to know God's love and acceptance of them.
We long for all those in pain and distress
to be comforted and relieved.

Silence

God our Father:
let your kingdom come.

We long for the dying to recognise
their need of God and his power to save;
for those who have died to be judged with mercy
and rest in God's peace.

Silence

God our Father:
let your kingdom come.

We give you thanks, Lord God,
for your teaching and your example
which opens our eyes to your truth.

Merciful Father,
**accept these prayers
for the sake of your Son,
our Saviour Jesus Christ. Amen.**

PROPER 21

Sunday between 25 September and 1 October inclusive

*Wealth can make us complacent so that we fail
to notice the needs of those around us.*

All our needs are God's concerns.
Let us pray to him now.

Father, make us a listening Church,
welcoming to the hesitant,
encouraging to the young,
sensitive to the differences and attentive to the needs.

Silence

God, in mercy:
hear us as we pray.

Father, make us a caring world,
wise in government,
honest in promises,
far-sighted in the management of resources,
and open-hearted in charitable giving.

Silence

God, in mercy:
hear us as we pray.

Father, make us a responsible community,
supporting our neighbours and friends,
sharing one another's sorrows and joys,
and opening our homes to your indwelling.

Silence

God, in mercy:
hear us as we pray.

Father, as we remember those
who have asked for our prayers,
take their needs and provide for them,
take their wounds and heal them,
take their suffering and comfort them.

Silence

God, in mercy:
hear us as we pray.

Father, as we call to mind those who have died,
may they know the welcoming of your love
into eternal joy.

Silence

God, in mercy:
hear us as we pray.

Thank you, Holy God,
for knowing our needs
even before we become aware of them ourselves.

Merciful Father,
accept these prayers
for the sake of your Son,
our Saviour Jesus Christ. Amen.

Proper 22

Sunday between 2 and 8 October inclusive

*God hears our distress and our crying,
and feels it with us.*

Knowing that God hears our prayers,
let us share our concerns with him
for the Church and for the world.

Father, we pray for all in lay and ordained ministry,
as they labour for the growth of your kingdom on earth;
keep them strong in the faith,
provide them with the energy and resources they need,
and inspire them daily with your love.

Silence

Lord, you are our hope:
you are our strength.

We pray for all meetings, conventions, and conferences,
for all policy making and planning;
may delicate negotiations be sensitively led,
and painful decisions bravely and wisely taken.

Silence

Lord, you are our hope:
you are our strength.

We pray for those we have upset or angered,
and those who have upset or angered us;
we pray for those who worry us,
and those we love but seldom manage to see.

Silence

Lord, you are our hope:
you are our strength.

We pray for those who are far from home
and those for whom it is too dangerous to return home;
we pray for the lonely, the unhappy,
those in pain and those convalescing.

Silence

Lord, you are our hope:
you are our strength.

We remember those who have come
to the end of their earthly life,
and for those whose lives feel bleak
and empty without them.
We pray for mercy and peace and comfort.

Silence

Lord, you are our hope:
you are our strength.

Thank you, Lord, for being there beside us
through all the dark and rocky places in our lives.

Merciful Father,
**accept these prayers
for the sake of your Son,
our Saviour Jesus Christ. Amen.**

PROPER 23

Sunday between 9 and 15 October inclusive

*God can always use even seemingly
hopeless situations for good.*

God has proclaimed his love for us.
We can trust him with all our cares and concerns.

Lord, heal the Church of all its splits and divisions,
and bless its growth towards unity;
heal it of all unhealthy introspection
and bless its commitment to loving outreach.

Silence

Have pity on us, Lord:
you alone can save us.

May our society be mindful of those
who have particular difficulties;
may our laws testify to our sense of justice,
honour and integrity;
may the world's leaders be wisely advised
and honestly motivated.

Silence

Have pity on us, Lord:
you alone can save us.

Walk about our homes with your gifts of peace,
patience, forgiveness and joy;
help us through the disappointments and tragedies,

and celebrate with us in all our festivities,
for you are our most honoured guest.

Silence

Have pity on us, Lord:
you alone can save us.

We pray for all suffering from leprosy
and other infectious and life-threatening diseases;
Give courage to the long-term and chronically ill
and give respite to those who are at their wits' end.

Silence

Have pity on us, Lord:
you alone can save us.

We remember those who have died,
and we think of their loved ones, who miss them.
May this earthly death be a birth
into the eternal joy of heaven.

Silence

Have pity on us, Lord:
you alone can save us.

With great thankfulness we praise you
for your constant faithfulness to us,
your recognition of our deepest thoughts,
and your desire for our healing and wholeness.

Merciful Father,
accept these prayers
for the sake of your Son,
our Saviour Jesus Christ. Amen.

PROPER 24

Sunday between 16 and 22 October inclusive

*Don't get side-tracked;
always pray and don't give up.*

Our help comes from the Lord.
Let us pray to him now.

Loving Father, we pray for those
who teach prayer and Bible study
at schools and colleges, retreat houses, and conferences,
and in churches and homes all over the world.
We pray that many will find your words
speaking into their situation
and providing the guidance they need.

Silence

Lord, we love your ways:
our help comes from you.

We pray for those picking their way
through situations of potential conflict and danger;
for law makers and keepers
and all who are oppressed unjustly;
for the leaders of the nations and their people.

Silence

Lord, we love your ways:
our help comes from you.

We pray for the grace to listen to one another
and respond to one another's needs;

we pray for a spirit of co-operation and generosity
in our homes and neighbourhoods.

Silence

Lord, we love your ways:
our help comes from you.

We pray for those who are wrestling with problems
which seem too big to cope with;
for those who have recently received news
that has stunned or appalled them,
and are still in a state of shock.

Silence

Lord, we love your ways:
our help comes from you.

We pray for those who have gone through death,
that they may be judged with mercy
and brought safely into the eternal life of heaven.

Silence

Lord, we love your ways:
our help comes from you.

Loving Father, we thank you
for your constant faithfulness to us
in spite of our tendency to fall far short
of our responsibilities.

Merciful Father,
accept these prayers
for the sake of your Son,
our Saviour Jesus Christ. Amen.

PROPER 25

Sunday between 23 and 29 October inclusive

When we recognise our dependence on God
we will approach him with true humility
and accept his gifts with joy.

Let us pray to the God who made us and sustains us.

Look with mercy on your Church,
with all our faults and failings,
missed opportunities and misunderstandings,
as we learn to be truly your body on earth.

Silence

God of our making:
have mercy on us.

We lay before you the political issues,
the moral dilemmas and the dreams of peace
that concern our world,
and all who share its resources.
Where we can see no clear way forward
give us your vision and enable us
to be good stewards of all you provide.

Silence

God of our making:
have mercy on us.

We ask you to take all our relationships
and drench them in your transforming love,
so that we appreciate one another more,
and value what each has to offer.

Silence

God of our making:
have mercy on us.

Surround with comfort and reassurance
those who feel spiritually dried-up
or emotionally drained;
heal and mend broken bodies and broken hearts,
and provide clear pools of water for those
who are walking the valley of misery and depression.

Silence

God of our making:
have mercy on us.

Gather into your kingdom
those who have run the race
and fought the good fight,
and have mercy on all who are at the point of death.

Silence

God of our making:
have mercy on us.

We give you thanks and praise
for the wideness of your mercy,
and the personal attention
of your provision for us.

Merciful Father,
**accept these prayers
for the sake of your Son,
our Saviour Jesus Christ. Amen.**

ALL SAINTS' DAY

Sunday between 30 October and 5 November inclusive

In Christ we are chosen to be God's holy people.

Let us pray to the God
who can love sinners into saints.

Thank you, Father, for the faithful prayers
of so many over the generations;
for the lifetimes of quiet godliness;
for the struggles bravely borne
and the witness of strong faith.

Silence

Make us all:
worthy of our calling.

Thank you, Father, for all peace-makers
and those who strive for justice and reconciliation;
thank you for those who work to relieve suffering
and manage the world's resources more fairly.

Silence

Make us all:
worthy of our calling.

Thank you for the blessing and hope
of each new generation;
for the richness of good friendships,
the happiness of those in love,
and the comfort of prayer support.

Silence

Make us all:
worthy of our calling.

Thank you for the care and attention
given to those in pain and ill health;
for the example of those
whom it is always a pleasure to visit,
in spite of their suffering;
for those who allow their suffering
to be used for some good.

Silence

Make us all:
worthy of our calling.

Thank you for the love and encouragement
we have received through the years
from those who have died in faith
and are remembered with great affection.

Silence

Make us all:
worthy of our calling.

Thank you for all the saints of heaven
who join us as we praise God
in all his holiness.

Merciful Father,
**accept these prayers
for the sake of your Son,
our Saviour Jesus Christ. Amen.**

FOURTH SUNDAY BEFORE ADVENT

Sunday between 30 October and 5 November inclusive*

* For use if the Feast of All Saints was celebrated on
1 November and alternative propers are needed.

*Jesus came to search out the lost and save them. Through
   him we come to our senses and make our lives clean.*

Let us still ourselves in our Father's presence
and tell him what is on our hearts.

Loving Father, look into us and teach us
to know ourselves more honestly,
to recognise the areas which need cleansing,
and rejoice in the work you have done
in our lives as individuals
and as the people of God.

Silence

Lord, may our lives:
express our love for you.

Fill Parliament and all places of government
throughout the world
with a desire for integrity and a determination
to stamp out corruption and deceit.
Guide all who lead and all who advise.

Silence

Lord, may our lives:
express our love for you.

Speak your peace and reconciliation
into all family disputes and hurtful misunderstandings;
nurture a spirit of loving community
in our neighbourhood,
and heighten our awareness of one another's needs.

Silence

Lord, may our lives:
express our love for you.

Bring reassurance and practical help
to those who are close to despair;
support those in long-term suffering
and use us as instruments of your healing love.

Silence

Lord, may our lives:
express our love for you.

Welcome into your kingdom
those who have faithfully lived out their days;
as we miss their physical presence,
we thank you for the gift of their lives.

Silence

Lord, may our lives:
express our love for you.

As today you have strengthened our resolve
to put our lives right with you,
we thank you for alerting us to dangers
and providing the courage to change.

Merciful Father,
**accept these prayers
for the sake of your Son,
our Saviour Jesus Christ. Amen.**

THIRD SUNDAY BEFORE ADVENT

Sunday between 6 and 12 November inclusive

*Life after death is not wishful thinking
but a definite reality.*

Let us pray to the great God of heaven
who stands among us now.

Heavenly God, as the earthly part of your Church
we come before you with our thanks and praise
for your living presence among us,
in our worship together
and in our separate times of prayer.
We thank you for bringing the joy of heaven to earth
as you lift us into your presence.

Silence

You are our God:
living for ever and ever.

Look with mercy on our world
as we work out policies and target needs,
and misunderstand one another's cultures
and get carried away with excesses
and the taste of power.

Silence

You are our God:
living for ever and ever.

May our waking, working, eating, relaxing and sleeping
become a pattern coloured and lit by your love;
may our homes reflect it,

our places of work be energised by it,
and our relationships glow with it.

Silence

You are our God:
living for ever and ever.

To those who are losing heart
give your heavenly encouragement and patience;
to the young and vulnerable
give heavenly protection;
to the ill and the damaged
give heavenly healing and inner peace,
as you touch our lives with yours.

Silence

You are our God:
living for ever and ever.

Knowing that physical death
is not the end of life,
but the beginning of a new dimension,
we recall our loved ones who have died
and commend them to your eternal keeping.

Silence

You are our God:
living for ever and ever.

As you fill our hearts with heavenly joy
we pour out our love and praise
to you, our living God!

Merciful Father,
**accept these prayers
for the sake of your Son,
our Saviour Jesus Christ. Amen.**

SECOND SUNDAY BEFORE ADVENT

Sunday between 13 and 19 November inclusive

*There will be dark and dangerous times as
the end approaches, but by standing firm
through it all we will gain life.*

The Lord is always ready to listen;
let us pray to him now.

Lord, we pray particularly for those
whose faith is being battered
and those who no longer pray;
we pray for our training programmes
and our weekly worship;
for our faith to be deepened and strengthened.

Silence

Keep us faithful:
firm to the end.

We pray for those whose responsibility it is
to manage the world's economy,
and for those who have difficult
ethical decisions to make;
we pray for wisdom and courage to do what is right.

Silence

Keep us faithful:
firm to the end.

We pray for the world our children will inherit
and ask your blessing on all parents
and the responsibilities they face;

we ask for understanding, maturity,
and the gift of laughter.

Silence

Keep us faithful:
firm to the end.

We pray for the victims of disasters,
famines, earthquakes and plagues;
for all who are crying
and those who have no tears left.
We pray for comfort, renewed strength,
and available friends.

Silence

Keep us faithful:
firm to the end.

We pray for those who are nearing death
and those who have died;
especially we pray for those
who have died suddenly and unprepared.
We pray for mercy and forgiveness.

Silence

Keep us faithful:
firm to the end.

We give you thanks, Lord God,
that you always provide the grace we need
to accomplish what you ask of us.

Merciful Father,
accept these prayers
for the sake of your Son,
our Saviour Jesus Christ. Amen.

CHRIST THE KING

Sunday between 20 and 26 November inclusive

*This Jesus, dying by crucifixion between criminals,
is the anointed King of all creation
in whom all things are reconciled.*

Through Jesus, our King, let us pray.

As we celebrate Jesus, the head of the Church body,
we pray for all the members
with their various gifts and ministries;
we pray that even our weaknesses
can be used to your glory
for the good of the world.

Silence

Christ is the image:
of the invisible God we worship.

May all monarchs and heads of state
be led in ways of truth and righteousness,
and recognise with humility
that they are called to serve.
We pray for all shepherds,
rescue teams and trouble-shooters;
for all who work to recover the lost.

Silence

Christ is the image:
of the invisible God we worship.

May we reach out to one another
with greater love and better understanding;

we pray for our homes, our relatives,
our neighbours and our friends,
particularly those who do not yet realise
the extent of your love for them.

Silence

Christ is the image:
of the invisible God we worship.

May those who have been scattered
far from their homes and loved ones
be enabled to live again in peace and happiness;
may the bitter and resentful find hope again
and the confused find new direction.

Silence

Christ is the image:
of the invisible God we worship.

May the dying know your closeness,
and those who mourn their loved ones
know for certain that your kingdom
stretches across both sides of death.

Silence

Christ is the image:
of the invisible God we worship.

Our hearts are filled with thanksgiving
as we realise again
the extraordinary extent of your love for us.

Merciful Father,
**accept these prayers
for the sake of your Son,
our Saviour Jesus Christ. Amen.**